*History is not just stone, notable people, and bricks. It includes the reaction of those who were there and the community's ongoing response."*

—Jim Boles

Vanishing Past Series
This book is part of the Vanishing Past Series published by Vanishing Past Press LLC. Vanishing Past Press is dedicated to the documentation, preservation, and distribution of works of scholarship and cultural importance with emphasis on under examined or unexplored topics. This book is part of that effort.

Copyright © 2020, James M Boles

All rights reserved. No part of this publication may be reproduced, stored in a retrieval system, or transmitted in any form by any process—electronic, mechanical, photocopying, recording, or otherwise—without the prior written permission of the copyright owner. For reprint permission information, please contact jamesboles47@gmail.com.

Published by: Vanishing Past Press
Layout design: Rachel Bridges
Director of Technical Services: Carolyn Ryer

Cover image: Boot Leg Spring, Artist Jeff Watkins - Lockport, New York

ISBN: 978-1-949860-02-3

STORIES FROM THE SPRINGS

The Niagara Frontier

James M. Boles

Editor's Note: The exact language of this time has been retained for historical accuracy. No offense is intended toward any individual or group.

Table of Contents

Introduction 1

Chapter One: Boot Leg Spring 9

Chapter Two: The Devil's Cave Springs 15

Chapter Three: Hollow Log Salt Spring 23

Chapter Four: Crapsey House Springs 37

Chapter Five: The Springs on Cold Springs Road 43

Chapter Six: The Puzzle of Local Mineral Springs 47

Chapter Seven: Vita Water Spring 53

Chapter Eight: Sulphur Springs Hotel
in Pendleton, New York 59

Chapter Nine: The Stella Niagara Grotto Spring 65

Chapter Ten: The Joe Whalen Sulfur Spring 69

Chapter Eleven: Springs and Artesian Wells
in Royalton, New York 73

Chapter Twelve: Springs You Can Visit
in Niagara County 79

Chapter Thirteen: Are the Springs Dry? 89

Chapter Fourteen: Chief Joseph Brant's Spring 93

Author's Notes 103

Introduction

I became interested in springs while researching the book *They Did No Harm—Alternative Medicine in Niagara Falls, NY*, exploring the alternative medicine available during the era Niagara Falls was a healthful spa town (roughly from the 1830s to the 1930s).

The abundant spring water was regarded as a medicine for cures and healing. That is where my recent involvement started. As a child, I drank from springs in Lockport, New York, on Hawley Street Hill, Garden Street, and Glenwood Ave—and the water did taste good. As I uncovered each spring, the stories poured out. Through these springs, we discover a unique history of the Niagara Frontier. The water does not go away unless changed by man. Usually the springs remain to tell

Historical Monteagle Springs Sanitarium, Niagara Falls, New York.

their story. In the 1800s, there was much interest in the minerals and mineral water of the recently settled Niagara Frontier. Here are a few examples from *Mineralogy of New York* by Lewis C. Beck, MD (1842) and *The United States Geological Survey, Lists and Analysis of Mineral Springs* by Albert C. Peale, MD (1886).

> SULPHUREOUS: at Lockport on the Towawanda Creek, two miles from the village. (These springs would have a large amount of Sulphur).
>
> CHALYBEATE: miles North of Lewiston, on the farm of Capt. Leonard several others in the vicinity. (These springs would have a large amount of iron salts).
>
> BRINE: Several along the course of Eighteen-mile creek, between Lockport and Lake Ontario. (These springs would have a large amount of salt).
>
> INFLAMMABLE GAS: At Gasport, in the town of Royalton, 6 1/2 miles from Lockport.

Mineralogy of New York: 1842, Niagara.

> Lockport Mineral Spring.one mile North of Lockport, Niagara County saline improved, but used by the residents of Lockport. There is a further analysis of this spring, listing the tested content of Sodium Chloride (salt) at (111.42 grains per gallon).
>
> Sulphur Spring: North part of Pendleton NY Township

From the Department of the Interior, United States Geological Survey No.32: 1886-New York State.

These two government documents list known springs and, in some cases, the mineral content or use of the water. They were looking at the commercial application of the water because at that early and primitive time in science, medicine, and healing, the minerals were thought to assist with health problems—and some may have. I still use these publications, because they are useful in tracking down old springs and give us a perspective of the importance of springs in earlier times.

A look at the mineral content shows local springs contained ingredients that had healing potential: bicarbonate of soda used for stomach, digestion, and coughs; lithium used for mood disorders; salt used for wounds and mouth sores; and other minerals that may have been helpful. The springs were also used to supplement well and city water when they were deemed contaminated, and they were often commercialized with the bottled water sold as a healthy alternative to other water sources. Local breweries advertised their use of spring water to show the purity of their beer.

In early accounts of the Niagara Frontier, the springs along the major routes are mentioned as both geographic references and as rest areas. There is a pattern of discovery by early travelers and settlers, and their reports mention Native Americans using the springs. Many of the Native American footpaths that became our present roads led to springs or had springs along the way, providing water for travelers and animals.

Improvements in the Springs

Often the first improvement to a spring would be an open basin to hold the water for drinking; hands, cups, and buckets were used to dip into the water. This left the water vulnerable to the spread of bacteria and diseases from animal and human contact. Then there was one major change that reduced the contaminates that were entering the water. The basin was covered, protecting it from external contamination, and the water ran out of a pipe. Visitors could then use the spring with reduced danger.

How are springs viewed by the public? The articles and presentations about springs attract the interested public. People want to know about the springs they remember as children. They quietly want to

Ladies drinking from cups at the covered Goat Island Spring, Niagara Falls, New York. Files of J. Boles.

know if it is still there, flowing, and they always remark about the good taste: "It's the best water I ever had."

The Magic of Springs

I received several phone calls from an elderly man who read one of my articles about springs and insisted upon speaking to me. He said he had been drinking from the local springs for over seventy years. He claimed to have the stamina of a forty-year-old and mentioned for proof, I should "just ask the ladies." His final statement to me was, "The government is trying to take away our free water."

I met a couple who moved near a well-known spring because she had a serious illness. They claimed that frequently drinking the water, over the years, has cured her.

High on the Niagara escarpment is a vigorous spring that is claimed to bring good luck if you drink from it three days in a row. Named

"Good Luck Spring," it is high up on a wet, muddy cliff, and it would be hard work; good luck making it up there three days in a row.

In a small hamlet by a lake, I was invited by a longtime resident to look at a pond and the spring that kept it full.

Good Luck Spring, Lewiston, New York. Files of Scott Ensminger, the Falz Guy.

The spring water now returned into the pond; the pipe was gone, and there was no external water. This spring, on the bank of the pond, was once the center of the neighborhood, like a town well. It had been gone for many years, but some remembered it. I visited this pond on an early summer day. There were several yard sales, so people were out. Those who remembered the mineral water claimed that there were many medical cures: cancer, headaches, hangovers. People came from miles away to drink it, stating that the water tasted good and had an ample flow. Even the "newcomers" knew about the former spring and the pond.

Now that the spring water is in the pond, the pond now has some of this magic. Local lore has it that the pond can predict the weather in the lake. As goes the pond, so goes the Lake. Although some distance from the lake residents think that the pond is connected to the lake underground. The pond never dries up; it is always full. The last story holds that a liquor running boat sunk into the pond and is still there full of prohibition rum. The spring-fed pond did connect to the lake in the past.

The springs in this book have had a long history. The water from many of them was used for healing in facilities and sold as healthy drinks with medical claims. The water of quite a few was used for brewing beer.

Note on Visiting the Springs

Many of the springs described in this book are on private property, and you may need permission; often there will be posted signs. I have tried to indicate if the springs can be visited, but access often changes. The water quality varies and can change quickly. The water needs to be tested before use. I have tested most of the springs with a well test kit; the water quality is good in some, and a few are contaminated.

James Boles, EdD, is a Lockport, New York, native and retired CEO of People Inc., a Western New York health and human services organization. He received his doctorate in education from Columbia University. In 1998, he founded the Museum of disABILITY History, Buffalo New York and received the Hervey B. Wilber Historic Preservation Award for his work with the museum. Under President George W. Bush, he was appointed for two terms on the President's Committee for People with Intellectual Disabilities. Now retired, Boles lectures and writes about the past. He has a strong interest in preserving the area's history and promoting cultural tourism. This publication is one of a series that will look at our past produced by Vanishing Past Press. The purpose of Vanishing Past Press is to encourage, develop, publish, and market works of scholarship and cultural importance, with a focus on under examined or unexplored history. Boles can be reached at Vanishing Past Press, jamesboles47@gmail.com.

Vanishing Past Press

Before I retired, I published under the "Abandoned History" Series from People Ink Press through the Museum of disABILITY History, Buffalo New York. I support all the efforts of this worthy organization. Now retired, I will be writing for Vanishing Past Press, whose corporate headquarters is located at one end of our family room.

Jim Boles testing a seep for salt. Photo by Norm LaJoie, Hartland, New York, Historian.

CHAPTER 1

Bootleg Spring

Springs show up in the early history of Niagara County because they were landmarks and resting areas on the early trails. These routes through the Niagara Frontier were often Native American footpaths with springs along the way for the travelers and their animals. The springs were well known along the main trails, such as the Old Niagara Trail, which included Chestnut Ridge Road from Batavia, New York, past Charles Wilber's log tavern on Cold Springs Road and onto Stone Road, meeting Route 104 (Ridge Road) at Warrens' Corners and West to Lewiston and Fort Niagara.

A man named John Street was murdered in 1790 while camped at a spring near Ridge Road (Route 104), a mile west of Warrens Corners, New York. John Street, a Fort Niagara businessman, was traveling to Massachusetts and was rumored to be carrying a large sum of money.

Boot Leg Spring, as interpreted by Lockport, New York, artist Jeff Watkins 2019.

At that time, Ridge and connecting roads were nothing more than paths; they were dangerous with frequent robberies. After John Street's death, travelers camped at the spring found some remains when their dog retrieved a boot with an attached leg. Scraps of John Street's clothing were found hanging in the bushes a year later. The men responsible for the murder and robberies were shortly thereafter captured. From an account:

> In 1790 after I had sold a drove of cattle at Lewiston (to go over the river), and at Fort Niagara I met with John Street, the father of the late Samuel Street, of Chippewa, C.W. He was going to Massachusetts and said he would like my company through the wilderness, as far as Geneva. Waiting a few days, and he had not [been] getting ready, I started without him. He followed in a few days and was murdered at a spring, near the Ridge Road, a mile west of Warren's." Judge Hopkins went on to say, "His friends in Canada, gathered up fragments of the body, and carried them home for burial. He was robbed of a considerable sum of money.

For now, given the details, I am going to name the spring "Boot Leg Spring." The exact location of the spring is unknown; however, the account has it one mile west of Warrens Corners (which was Forsyth Corners) and the historic Forsyth Tavern in Cambria, New York. This story is from the *Pioneer History of the Holland Purchase of Western New York,* 1852, by O. Turner as told by Judge Hopkins.

It is hard to imagine, but in the year 1790, Ridge Road (Route 104) was a primitive trail. The Forsyth Tavern was not yet open, and for many travelers camping was the only option. Ridge Road heading east after Warrens Corners was often not used because of the swampy conditions, although it was often navigable in the winter when the water was frozen. An alternative for those heading east was to use Stone Road, which also had a junction at Forsyth Corners (now Warrens Corners). This is where Route 93 meets Route 104 in the town of Cambria, New York.

Entrance to Forsyth Tavern on Ridge Road, Cambria, New York.

Restored Forsyth Tavern, 5182 Ridge Road at Warrens Corners, Cambria, New York.

Update, July 2019: I handed out a "Wanted" flyer in Cambria, New York, during a recent "town wide yard sale." Homes, businesses, and churches were open along Route 104 (Ridge Road) and invited the public to look at their sale items. I passed out the Information about Boot Leg Spring and left "Wanted" flyers, hoping that someone might know the location of the spring. There was considerable interest. I have received three calls and several emails with possible sites. A spring behind the cemetery on Budd Road was reported by a nearby farmer, and the local mailman called with additional information.

I received a detailed account from Richard McIntosh. As a child, he lived on a farm with his family in Cambria, about one mile west of Warrens Corners at 4931 Ridge Road. The well on his farm was known to be spring-fed and was praised by visitors for its taste. Mr. McIntosh and I are going to visit the farm in the spring.

Northeast Cambria Union Cemetery, Budd Road, Cambria, New York. A spring has been reported behind the cemetery.

The Forsyth Tavern 1808

I am using the restored Forsyth Tavern in Cambria, New York, and the related Jay Bird Antiques shop in the tavern barn as my base of operations because they are the closest active business to the spring and have been very helpful with my search. The tavern and the barn were just restored, are in use, and there are plans to further prepare the site as a tourist destination. The Forsyth Tavern just received a listing on the National Register of Historic Places and has applied for a provisional charter to the Regents of New York State to be a museum. Posted on the wall in the Jay Bird Antiques barn for customers to see is my "Wanted" poster for the Boot Leg Spring. Tyler Booth is the knowledgeable proprietor of the Forsyth Tavern, and his father, Jay Booth, operates the antique shop. Both are available to answer customers' questions about local history and field information about Boot Leg Spring or other springs along the old road. Readers with questions or information can contact Jim Boles at jamesboles47@gmail.com.

I would like to thank Tyler Booth of the Forsyth Tavern and Tom Collister, curator of the Lewiston, New York, History Museum, for their assistance with this chapter.

CHAPTER 2

The Devil's Cave
Lockport, New York

Are the springs on the escarpment in the city of Lockport, New York, linked to the Lockport Cave? Many springs are located along the escarpment, which runs roughly east to west. In early reports (1820s–1890s) of Lockport's history, accounts of a large cave system are mentioned, referring to it as Devil's Cave. This cave runs along the escarpment and has water running into it. As one of the explorers in the 1960s–1970s, I can confirm that there were fresh

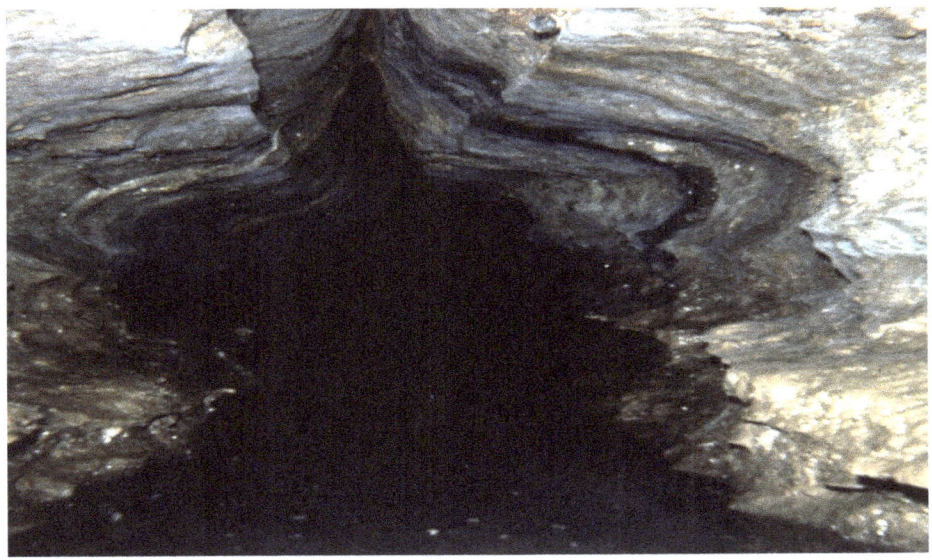

This section of the Devil's Cave is under the city of Lockport, New York, now renamed Culvert Cave. Photo from the files of Scott A. Ensminger, copyright 1984, Hazlitt Krog.

streams of water running through the section we crawled through with its many side passages. As the history is reviewed, there may be a connection to the cave system and many of the springs. There is little doubt that under the streets and houses of Lockport, a cave exists. Craig Bacon, Deputy Niagara County Historian, thoroughly documented the cave's long history in his January 8, 2012, *Buffalo News* article showing evidence that the cave remains in place and that it was never fully explored.

J Boles 2016

Cave Street, Lockport, New York, named after the mysterious Lockport cave in 1834. The cave is found below.

Accounts in historian Bacon's article mention streams flowing through the cave. It is likely that the cave was formed in the rock by the rush of water in underground streams, springs, overflow from nearby Eighteen-Mile Creek, and spillway activity from the ancient lakes.

When the Lockport Cave Co. was formed in the 1880s, the intent was to open the cave for a tourist attraction. As the cave was prepared for use, bridge work on nearby Eighteen-Mile Creek caused water to enter the cave. The large volume of flooding went on for several days as Eighteen-Mile Creek poured into the cave. It was never discovered where the water drained as it vanished down the cave. It did not appear in the canal or on or below the escarpment. The cave never opened as a tourist attraction.

In the June 3, 1970, *Niagara Falls Gazette* article titled: "Polluted Springs Laid to Search for Caverns," Reporter Gen Hammond of the Gazette Lockport Bureau covered the concerns by officials about the cave exploration and the pollution of springs. Robert N. Clark, senior environment health technician with the Niagara County Health Department mentioned that the health department had recently found two springs on the escarpment, Garden Street Spring at the foot of North Adam and Glenwood Spring in the Gulf off Glenwood Avenue, that were polluted. Mr. Clark went on to state:

> These kids have been exploring into some of the city's sewers in search of an opening into the caves. We don't know where these springs originate or where they empty. It could be the youngsters have fouled up the sewers and possible laterals to the caves and have contaminated the springs.

The article also made public that City Engineer William C. Gerner had issued orders that prohibited further search into the cave or explorations in the city's sewer system unless a bond was posted at city hall.

The author, Jim Boles, in the Lockport Cave in 1970 Lockport Union-Sun & Journal Files, Niagara County, New York, Historian's Office.

WRONG OF SPRING- Lockport residents Augustine Sansone and Jerome Porretta at the cemented-over cap of a natural spring in Lowertown. The water, once welcomed on hot summer days and for a time used in bottled spring water, is now polluted. Gazette photo by John Kudia. Niagara Falls Gazette January 7, 1976. Garden Street Spring is now closed off to the public. This spring was mentioned as connected to the Lockport Cave.

Garden Street Spring in the 1970s before its closure. Files Niagara County, New York, Historian's Office.

Glenwood Spring, Glenwood Avenue. *J. Boles 2016*

Is the mentioned Glenwood Spring also connected to the Lockport Cave System? This spring still flows and is frequently recalled by long-time Lockport residents who used the water for many years.

There are other links to the cave and the springs. In Clarence O. Lewis's (Niagara County Historian) 1965 article in the *Lockport Union-Sun & Journal*, there is a historical account that describes a cave channel that ran toward the Lockport Brewery, one of a succession of breweries located on Chestnut and Spring streets.

> The old cave the mouth of which was buried about 35 years ago, is supposed to have run in a direction almost due west (although there are tales that the cave curved after running west about 300 ft., and a lateral veered to the north and east and came out in the gulf near where the Lockport Brewery is located on Chestnut and Spring streets).

As reported by historian Ann Marie Linnabery in the October 21, 2017, *Lockport Union-Sun & Journal* the list of breweries includes Ulrich's Brewery, then Union Brewing Company, Lockport Brewing Company, and Lock City Brewing Company.

Jim Castle, a local resident and businessman who as a child used to explore in the abandoned Chestnut Street Brewery while attending nearby St. Joseph's School, stated in a 2015 interview, "The boys would sneak over to the old brewery building and in the south end of the basement there was a cave with a small stream running through it. We always thought it ran into the larger Lockport Cave."

Also, in the book *The Caves of Niagara County, New York*, there is mention of a link to the Lockport Cave System and Culvert Cave running near Stainthorp's Brewery on Spring and Chestnut Streets. The mapped section of Culvert Cave runs to the brewery property, which is located on the north and south side of Chestnut Street in

Lockport, New York. Spring Street and nearby Cold Spring Alley are in this area.

There are many questions about the cave. As usual with the mysterious Lockport Cave, there's always just enough evidence to keep us wondering and searching for answers to the unexplained.

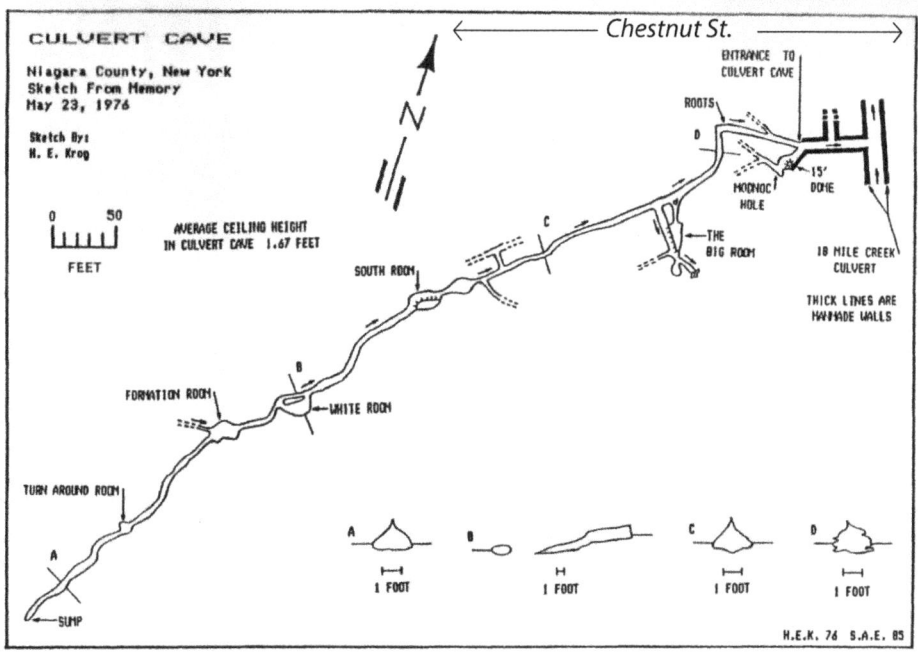

The entrance to the Culvert Cave is close to Chestnut and Spring Streets, Lockport, New York, near the Chestnut Street breweries. From The Caves of Niagara County, New York by Scott Ensminger.

CHAPTER 3

Hollow Log Salt Spring:
A Native American Salt Well
Somerset, New York

In the brush and trees of Somerset, New York, is an old salt spring believed to have been used by local Native Americans. Sitting quietly beside Fish Creek, the area is marked with the tracks of animals who have traveled there for the salt.

The town of Somerset, New York, the location of the Salt Spring.　　　*J. Boles 2019*

As the local history is told, this story dates back centuries to when a large, hollow Buttonwood tree was sunk eight feet into a salt seep, forming a well.

A faded picture from the files. The cleanup crew: L-R, Rev. Allyn Foster of Faith Methodist Church, Vernon Bateman, Edna Jerome, Lon McAdams II, and Herb Loesch, 1970s. Photo courtesy of the Somerset historian Peter Devereaux.

INDIAN SALT SPRING

When the white settlers first came to the Town of Somerset they found an Indian camping ground on the small stream now called Fish Creek, about three miles up from the mouth where it empties into Lake Ontario. The Indians camped there at all times during the year, but especially in the spring when the fish came up the creek to spawn. The Indians had chosen the camping ground because of a salt water spring which, in some seasons of the year, flowed out of the creek bed. In order to be sure of a plentiful supply of salt water the Indians dug down to the bed rock about 8 feet below the ground, and set a hollow buttonwood log down into the hole to create a shallow well. The log was hollowed out by burning the interior. The salt has preserved the wood so well that it is still in good condition all the way to the bottom.

Both Indians and whites continued to use the salt from the salt spring up until after the Civil War. Sometime before 1900 a small dam was put in the creek just below the spring and water backed up, covering all but the top of the well. People still living in Somerset can remember skating on the ice pond and circling the top of the salt well on their skates.

In 1967 a college class from Buffalo (Anthropology) camped at the site and dug trenches in the search for Indian relics. Many broken pieces of pottery were found and one French army uniform button. This led to speculation that either the French had camped there with Indians at some time prior to the American Revolution, or perhaps an Indian had purchased or stolen a French uniform from which the button was lost. Over the years many arrowheads and other Indian relics have been picked up in the fields adjacent to the salt spring.

A few years ago heavy spring storms caused a flood which tilted the buttonwood tree, and a group of Somerset citizens dug out around it and straightened it back up.

On July 4th, 1969, another group of townspeople gathered at the salt spring, rigged up a tripod, and set up a bucket brigade to empty and clean out the well. Several hundred pounds of mud, stones, sticks, etc. that people had thrown into the well for the past hundred years were shoveled up, hoisted out and dumped on the bank near the well. When emptied, the well filled up again at the rate of one gallon every five minutes. A gallon of the water was evaporated and yielded about a half-pound of salt, which indicates that the water is slightly less salty than sea water. When dry, the salt is colored a slightly brownish yellow.

Please do not throw anything into the well and help to keep it clean for other people who wish to see this old landmark.

SRM: lms

cc: Dr. Richard Brown
   Dr. Eric Brunger

History of the Salt Spring from the Barker/Somerset Historians Office, author Silas Molyneaux. Courtesy of Peter Devereaux, Somerset historian.

The local history, which has been passed on by the early settlers, who arrived about 1810, connects the Salt Log Well to the Native Americans who lived in the region. The story is that the first European settlers found the hollow log when they arrived. Although Native American artifacts have been dug at the site, it is also on a level bank of Fish Creek that may have been used for camping and fishing. The log has never been dated.

A check with Professor Doug Perrelli, director of the Archaeological Survey at the University of Buffalo, Buffalo New York, Dept. of Anthropology, uncovered an Archaeological Site File Checklist number 3553, which is an Archaeological Survey completed by the university. There was an identification of 1976, Clune & Johnson. The site was labeled as a Historic Euro-American (1810) salt well. The University of Buffalo Report 3553 does not support the use of the salt by Native Americans. The report states "The residents of the Town of Somerset believe that the well was established by Indians. This seems unlikely. The early Iroquois, who controlled this area in early historic times and who had close cultural affinities to the previous inhabitants, did not use salt and avoided the best salt spring in the area, at Syracuse, because they felt that it was inhabited by unfriendly spirits (Jesuit Relations 41: 123–125, 16 Aug 1654)." The report continues:

> The salt well is located on the south bank of Fish Creek, approximately 1200 feet WSW of the SW corner of the sewage treatment plant site. This well consists of a large hollow log resting vertically in a pool of salty water at the south edge of the creek. The log projects approximately 5 feet above the water and is approximately 4 feet in diameter. Previously a hand painted metal sign was attached to the log just above the water line. The sign said, 'Log placed here by Red men, oldest known well casing 1800-1962.' This sign is now obliterated.

The information is confusing. The account from the History of Niagara County, New York, 1878, Stanford and Co., states that the log was found by early settlers, circa 1810.

> About half a mile West or upstream from where Fish Creek crosses the road that runs from Somerset village to the Lake is a salt spring or well. There is or was a few years ago an old hollow button wood log sunk in the middle of the creek with one end just above the surface. This salt spring must have been operated by someone before the white settlers occupied the country as it has not been operated since 1810.

There are also reports that the salt well was not used from 1810 on, and another account that it was used by both Native Americans and settlers until about 1900, when a mill dam was built near Quaker Road flooding the spring area.

There was a time when there was little salt available in this region, and it is likely that the salt would have been valuable to both Native Americans and early settlers until 1825 when the canal boats brought salt from the Syracuse, New York, area. Salt wells would still be in use after 1825, because the salt was local and low or no cost.

There is an account of Native Americans catching fish in the streams, such as Fish Creek, that flow into Lake Ontario and bringing the fish back to Royalton, New York.

> One of the earliest settlers near Gasport was Jason Sawyer, who came from Vermont in 1816; his father came a short time later. Paul Sawyer built a cooper shop on the north bank of the gulf across the present water tower.
>
> There was a large fireplace in the shop, and each year this attracted Indians from the reservation on their way to fish on

Lake Ontario. They would stay the night in the shop, each one sleeping with his feet toward the fire; a day or two later, the squaws followed. On the return, the squaws laden with the fish that had been caught and dried, the braves followed a few days later.

Note that this story mentions that the fish were dried for preservation. This account is from the "Oral Histories of the Town of Royalton" and was forwarded to me by Jesse Bieber, the town historian.

The history records European explorers in the Niagara region as early as the 1600s and the first settlers in the Somerset area in 1810. The many uses of salt would be common knowledge, and information about it would have been exchanged.

Conclusion

Consultation with experts and further research indicates that Native Americans in upstate New York have left no historical record of the use of salt for preservation prior to 1810; however, there were references for its use for trading. So, it is likely that the Somerset Salt Well was created for extraction of salt for trading long before the European settlers arrived in the Somerset, New York, area circa 1810. The oral history from Somerset's first settlers is correct, and trading is the reason the salt well would have been in use before the settlers arrived.

How Old Is the Salt Well Log?

One option for determining the age of the Buttonwood log that forms the salt well is to use various scientific dating methods. Although I am in the process of obtaining the necessary permissions, the process was not completed before publication. However, I was able to use another dating process, devised by the International Society of Arboriculture, that involves measurements of the tree trunk and referencing a growth guide for the Buttonwood tree, also known as the American Sycamore. The Buttonwood tree is unique in that it hollows out as it ages. There are also Buttonwood trees found in the forest surrounding the salt spring.

J. Boles 2020

On the trail to the Hollow Log Salt Spring there are other Buttonwood trees. Here is one just as you start up the trail, to the South, labeled by a local historical group.

According to calculations, the salt well tree trunk was 162 years old when cut down. Using conservative figures, it was in the well in 1810, when it was discovered by early European settlers, and at that point it would be at least 162 years of age. Add in the 210 years that have passed since it was first discovered by settlers in 1810, and the Buttonwood log is at least 372 years of age. It also likely had been in the ground many years before 1810, which would add years to the dating. The log is well preserved by the salt.

Lorraine Wayner, Somerset historian, at the salt well 2005. Files of the Somerset, New York, Historians Office.

Respectful visitors can visit this spring. It is located just North of Barker, New York, on Quaker Road just before Lower Lake Road. There is a historical marker North of the bridge over Fish Creek on the west side of the road; follow the signs and marked trail.

J. Boles 2019

This sign is found on Quaker Road North of Barker, New York. Historical Marker placed by the Somerset Historical Society. The trail is to the right.

Entrance to the Salt Spring trail. *J. Boles 2019*

The trail to the Salt Spring is marked with white paint.   *J. Boles 2019*

Follow the marked trees. At a clearing where the marked trees end, turn left toward the creek and cross a small bridge over the creek. The Salt Spring is straight ahead.

As you walk the trail west, look to your left at the valley that the Fish Creek flows through. This area was once dammed as the whole ravine was a large mill pond for the mill on Quaker road near the bridge.

J. Boles 2019
The Salt Spring was converted into a well with a large hollow log sunk into the ground. Note the many animal prints.

Interior of salt well. The wood is bleached white from the salt.   *J. Boles 2019*

The well is still there. On a recent visit, a bucket of thick brine was scooped up.

J. Boles 2019
One gallon of brine from the salt well when boiled down produced a full quart of salt.

How to Spot a Salt Spring

The salt wells or springs in Niagara County are usually seeps that were found by locating a barren muddy spot with many animal tracks, often deer and racoon, with little vegetation. Salt was precious and costly in the region before the large salt discoveries were found in the Syracuse area shipped up the Erie Canal. These local salt deposits were sought after, and early explorers and surveyors marked the salt seeps for development. The seep was then hand dug out into a well and the brine was boiled down to produce the valuable salt.

In 1804, a large commercial salt operation was located on Wicks Road (was Salt Road) in the Town of Lockport, New York, which Lockport Town historian Larry Hasley and I located in 2016. The Wicks Road salt spring has been linked to surveyor Joseph Ellicott, who recorded the spring when he covered the area in the early 1800s.

Thanks to Lorraine Wayner, former historian of the Town of Somerset, New York, and to current historian Peter Devereaux for their time and information about the history of the salt spring.

CHAPTER 4

Crapsey House Springs
Sunset Drive, Lockport, New York

Located on the west side of what is now Sunset Drive, Lockport, New York, is a large stone house that was constructed circa 1845–1846. The first cabin on the property was built by Moses Crapsey in the 1830s, and initially the road was named for Mr. Crapsey but later changed to Sunset Drive.

The Crapsey farm in the 1870s from The History of Niagara County. *By Stanford & Company, 1878. From the files of Jean Linn, Town of Lockport, New York, historian.*

The historic house is now a beautifully restored home and a bed and breakfast for cats operated by Lin Sodja and Paul Bicker.

4878 Sunset Drive (The Crapsey House) built circa 1845–1846.   J. Boles 2015

The Niagara County Almshouse, which was built in 1829 on Niagara Street Extension, contracted with the Crapsey Farm to provide water, and in 1854, the county purchased additional land to accommodate the fittings and the hollow log pipes that conveyed the water to the Poor House and to the Almshouse grounds.

Log pipes were used in the 1800s. At first, they were bored by hand-operated augers. Later, with the invention of steam-powered augers, the process was more efficient.

Behind the house on the escarpment are several springs that were piped downhill to the Poor House on Niagara Street Extension. The drop from the springs on the escarpment to the Poor House foundation, according to the 1884 Lockport City Directory, was 140 feet.

Log Pipe, Salt Museum, Syracuse, New York. *J. Boles 2016*

J. Boles 2015
A strong clear stream still flows from the springs up on the hill.

Marker stone at entrance and right of way to poor house cemetery.   J. Boles 2015

The Almshouse Cemetery was restored in 2012 with the help of the Niagara County Department of Grounds, county historian Catherine Emerson, Orleans Monument Co., the Niagara County Sheriff's Department, People Inc., and many volunteers. Niagara County Legislature Chairman Bill Ross paved the way for the project for all the concerned groups involved. The cemetery is nicely maintained by the county. Stone foundations and a silo are all that remain of the large facility.

Thank you to Lin Sodja, Paul Bicker, Niagara County historian Catherine Emerson, and Jennifer Walkowski of the National Register of Historic Places, New York.

CHAPTER 5

The Springs on Cold Springs Road
Lockport, New York

I received an email from Geoffrey Harding, who was interested in the spring at Cold Springs Cemetery. He is researching a tale of the transportation of prisoners to Fort Niagara by Native Americans during the Revolutionary War. I passed onto him what I knew.

J. Boles 2017
Cold Springs Cemetery on Cold Springs Road. The site of genuine Niagara County history and many unsubstantiated legends.

Hartland town historian Norm Lajoie also asked about the spring at the corner of Cold Springs and Chestnut Ridge Roads. This area is the center of much early local history and many speculative tales; it does need more investigation. Ann Marie Linnabery wrote an excellent overview of the Cold Springs area for "Niagara Discoveries" in the November 15, 2014, edition of the *Lockport Union-Sun & Journal*, which can be accessed at www.lockportjournal.com.

One thing to be noted is that both roads, which were once early paths, have been rerouted, and deep depressions have been filled in so the locations may not be the same as in earlier times.

In my search for the spring, I saw water running out of the south bank of the cemetery on the southeast corner behind the remains of the DeSales school buildings that were razed in 1965. In 2012, Craig Kerrison, the Cold Springs Cemetery supervisor, said, "When the cemetery was expanded to the east, the stream was diverted into an underground pipe, the remnants of which can be seen in a couple of places." Kerrison indicated that the spring and its stream at one time ran through the cemetery, and because of flooding problems it was piped underground. It now runs under the length of the cemetery and exits near the railroad tracks to the north. As the cemetery employees go about their work, they sometimes run into it.

Kerrison also pointed out the close springs in the golf course, and it has been mentioned that in earlier times they may have also been part of the story. In a recent discussion with Linda Lee, a trustee of the cemetery board who is very knowledgeable about its history, it became clear that there could have been several springs along this early pathway.

Recently, working with Clifford Starke from the nearby Lockport Country Club, we discovered many springs throughout the Lockport Country Club. Starke is very knowledgeable about the property; he wrote an excellent history for a club publication. An early postcard of the club shows a spring house near the road (Route 31) with a stream running down the hill, and a pump house basin that was reportedly used by travelers on Route 31.

Springs along Route 31 near Cold Springs Road, Lockport Country Club, Lockport, New York. Files of J. Boles.

J. Boles 2017
A cold spring is found in the gully behind the old stone fence. Water still runs out of the south bank. Cold Springs Road, Lockport, New York.

CHAPTER 6

The Puzzle of Local Mineral Springs

Of all the subjects I write about in "Abandoned History," springs evoke the most interest. Each time I write about them, people call or email me with more information and their childhood memories. A lady called me about a spring she remembered from her childhood in Lockport, New York, that she believed to be near the end of McCue Street. She had been told by her family that the spring ran under her house. She remembered how good the water tasted. She had not seen the spring for many years and wondered if it was still there. I knocked on doors at the north end of McCue Street and found a homeowner who said she might know where it is located. It was on the far edge of her property on adjacent private land. This spring ran out of a rock outcropping on the escarpment, a beautiful park-like area, and I was told that it flowed a large amount of water in the spring. I was able to report back to my caller that the spring was still there.

However, I cannot always find the springs, because some are dry and reclaimed by nature, and many are on private property. There are still many springs that were important to early settlers and still used by residents into the 1970s. I have good historical research on dozens of interesting springs in Niagara County, and there are many more to find. With the help of the readers of the *Lockport Union-Sun & Journal*, I have received a couple of photographs and information about mineral springs that are believed to be in the area, but the photographs are not identified. The first image, contributed by a local resident, shows a man resting next to a stone bottling basin. This looks like the basin and stone mound that is in Rollin T. Grant Gulf Wilderness Park in Lockport, New York. The Lockport Mineral Spring was first commercialized in the 1860s, and the water was bottled and sold with medicinal claims.

Lockport Mineral Spring, Gulf Wilderness Park, Lockport, New York.

Stone Bottling Basin, Gulf Wilderness Park, Lockport, New York. *J. Boles 2015*

The second photo (below) was contributed by Joanne Ciraza, a Lockport resident who is interested in local history. Joanne first contacted the historians at the Niagara County Historical Society, who suggested that she show the picture to me. The photo was found in an old album. No additional information is available, but the other photographs in the album are local.

The photo is labeled "Mineral Springs," and the names Mary C., Minnie P., and Otto P. are written on the print. The man is drinking, and at his feet is a round basin.

I am also looking for more information on other springs mentioned to me by readers. Wally Edmister of Lockport, New York, has identified a spring, maybe an artesian well, on the corner of Block Church and Simms Roads in Royalton, New York. The spring is in an area of known artesian wells and springs. It is framed by a cement basin with a central flow pipe. Recent visits show a steady stream of water with a strong sulfur smell.

Other reported springs: Vince's Auto Yard, Route 93, Royalton, New York; off 104 Ridge Road, behind the cemetery on Budd Road, Cambria, New York; Spring Street Hill, Lockport, New York, on the northeast side of the bridge; Glenwood Avenue at Michigan Street; Route 104 at Purdy Road between Purdy and the creek. south side; Art Park Spring, Lewiston, New York; Good Luck Spring, Lewiston, New York; Spalding Spring, Lockport, New York, north of Main Street; Day Road, Lockport, New York; Eighteen-Mile Creek in Newfane on the banks of the creek; Wheeler Road, Newfane, New York. These all need further research, and, in some cases, they have to be located.

Do you know anything about these springs? Did you or your family members drink the water? I have heard many claims for good health and cures from drinking local spring water. Do you know of any stories?

Block Church Road Sulfur Spring, Royalton, New York. *J. Boles 2016*

CHAPTER 7

Vita Water Spring
Lockport, New York

At the east end of the city of Lockport just north of Route 31 (Main Street) is a path behind a picturesque tree-lined parkway that leads down to one of the more famous mineral springs, which operated as a commercial business for over eighty years.

Founded in 1916 by Lockport delicatessen owner James R. Rowe when the city issued Lockport Business License #017, Vita-Water made many health claims in local advertising. The strongest ads stated that the water would prevent death and typhoid fever, overcome bad feelings, and ward off germs and disease.

An analysis in 1923 reported the water was 100 percent pure with high levels of magnesium chloride (salt found in dry sea beds), calcium sulfate (salt), calcium carbonate (antacid), and six other minerals, including lithium bicarbonate, another salt that in a refined form is presently used to treat a mental health condition classified as bipolar disorder. It may seem that with all the salts in the mineral water it would taste salty; however, residents who drank the water said it was clear and refreshing.

Marketed as mineral water with health benefits, it was widely distributed to homes, businesses, restaurants, and health facilities in the greater Niagara County area. Vita-Water claimed to be "As pure as it's possible for water to be."

Will Philipps 2014

Vita Water Spring—Spring House and small stream. A drinking fountain for the golfers below was piped under the greens and available on the north bank, below the railroad tracks.

Spring House, Vita Spring.

J. Boles 2015

Vita Spring is a natural spring on a hill in what early locals called Rogers Grove. It poured out of the escarpment at a rate of up to 7,200 gallons a day, although the flow would slow in the summer and often have more bacteria after a heavy rain. In later years, the water was tested and treated.

At one time, run-off from the spring was used in an ice pond.

An interesting report, "Documents of the Assembly of the State of New York 1912 Report from the State Department of Health for the Year 1911," had many concerns about the water quality in Lockport, New York. However, Vita Water Spring was one of the few water sources that was praised: "The water from the Vita Spring shows a low bacterial count … and the water may be considered for suitability for domestic use."

The spring operated for over eighty years with only four owners. James R. Rowe started bottling in 1916. T. Bernard Rooney took over in 1930, and he was helped by Lockport fireman Bob Randall for twenty years. In the 1970s and 1980s, Warren Haseley owned the company. Doug Thompson took over the operation in the 1980s. He sold the customer list to Mayers Brothers Bottling in 1996, and the Vita-Water operation closed.

This article is a summary of over three years of research, and I would like to make the following acknowledgments: Interviews were conducted with local residents Tom McDonough, Jim Castle, and Jay Krull, along with Warren Haseley, former owner and operator (1970s–1980s); Bob Randall, retired fireman who phoned from his home in Virginia and recounted twenty years as a bottler and driver; and Doug Thompson, present owner and former operator in the 1980s–1990s. I'd also like to thank the Niagara County Historian's Office, the Lockport Library, the Niagara County Historical Society, and Will Philipps, University at Buffalo geologist and consultant.

A PURE SPRING WATER

VITA

For your protection, each VITA bottle is thoroughly cleaned before leaving the spring.

A new sterilized cork is inserted in each bottle, and a patented sanitary paper cap covers each cork and neck.

The water is delivered to you in an enclosed truck, thus eliminating dust, rain and road dirt.

When the water reaches you it is STILL a PURE Spring Water.

Our Motto:
SERVICE and SANITATION.

JAMES R. ROWE,

56 Cleveland Place,

Phone 227,   LOCKPORT, N. Y.

Lockport City Directory of 1930, p. 450. The Niagara County Historical Society has an early Vita Water cooler in its collection, Lockport, New York.

J. Boles 2015

Vita Water Processing Plant in rear of house—56 Cleveland Place, Lockport, New York. The barn and basement was used to clean and seal the bottles for preparation before delivery to customers.

J. Boles 2015

Wide Waters Restaurant, Lockport, New York. The Vita Spring stream flows behind the restaurant.

CHAPTER 8

Sulphur Springs Hotel
Pendleton, New York

Jim Sobczyk, a *Lockport Union-Sun & Journal* reader with a longtime interest in the history of Pendleton, called about the Sulphur Springs House, which was an 1850s hotel located in Pendleton on the banks of the Erie Canal. Jim mentioned that the building was being restored, so I quickly called the owner.

With holes in the roof and water damage sustained, the building's new owner, Joe Panepento, felt that it had to be rebuilt that year. "Another winter or two, it would be too far gone to save," he told me.

Joe and his crew from Pendleton-based JP Facility Services have been working for months to clean up the shacks and brush on the long-abandoned property. Joe should be credited with saving Sulphur Springs House, which he plans on making it into a residence after renovations are complete.

I have been researching this old Pendleton site for a number of years. Previous records about this early settlement and canal-traveler rest stop stated that the sulphur spring was located near the property. The area along the canal was known as Sulphur Springs, and the nearby canal lock was called the Sulphur Springs Guard Lock. The hotel was named Sulphur Springs House, identifying its general location.

"This steam shovel is shown working in the rock section of the Sulphur Springs Guard Lock." Photo courtesy of the Niagara History Center, Lockport, New York, provided by Alexa Gibney, marketing assistant.

It is not known whether the sulphur spring was on the hotel property or how the hotel offered the sulphur water as a healing aid for bathing and drinking. In the book *Pharmacy on the Niagara Frontier,* Laurence D. Lockie mentions, on page 158, that medicinal cures could be found at the hotel:

> However, in Pendleton, at the junction of the Bear Ridge with the Canal Road, there was at one time a Sulphur Springs Hotel, where people came to seek the curative powers of the springs. The residents of the hotel purchased their other remedies from the general stores in the vicinity.

In the 1836 *Gazette of the State of New York,* by T. F. Gorden, this mineral spring is mentioned:

> Near the canal, in the north part of the town, is a mineral spring impregnated with Sulphur and iron, supposed to possess some valuable curative powers, but its waters have not been analyzed.

In 2012, I discussed the spring and property with town historian Martin Gilbert. His thoughts were that "the Sulphur Springs Hotel was just a 'watering hole,' a regular bar for the locals and canalers." As he described the original building, "back then, the front porch wasn't enclosed and there wasn't a side porch at all."

J. Boles 2017

Joe Panepento, the new owner of the historic Pendleton Sulphur Springs Hotel.

Historic Pendleton Sulphur Springs Hotel.   *J. Boles 2017*

Pendleton Sulphur Springs Hotel.   *J. Boles 2019*

CHAPTER 9

The Stella Niagara Grotto Spring
Lower River Road,
Town of Lewiston, New York

On a rare dockable section of the Niagara River along an old path, which then became a roadway in Lewiston, the Stella Niagara Grotto Spring was well known and frequented by locals and travelers. The property has considerable early history; a natural landing on the river, it was used by Native Americans and then early travelers on the Niagara River. A historical marker in the front of the property details the story of the British in 1813 on their way to capture Fort Niagara using the riverfront landing for their boats.

Thanks to the help of Stella Niagara's archivist, Sister Mary Serbacki, I have been able to research the history of the spring. In 1902, the farmland was owned by F. R. March, and the water from the spring was sent to Dr. Herbert M. Hill of the University of Buffalo Chemical Laboratory for analysis. This would have been done because the mineral spring was thought to be a healing spring and may have been considered for commercialization. There is no information that its water was ever bottled, but there are several testimonies from users of the water. Dr. Sydney A. Dunham of Buffalo wrote in 1903, "I have used the Spring Water from the F. R. March's ... and find it a very fine water for family use. Pure and containing mineral matter which is good for the health and pleasant to the taste." John Piper, who also examined the spring, mentioned that "The spring is one of

[the] strongest springs in the Western Frontier and can develop a thousand barrels a day of absolutely pure water."

This spring must have been very vigorous, as 1,000 barrels is about 31,000 gallons, which seems very high, but it must have had an ample flow for bottling. Back then, the water would be tested for minerals, then that information would be considered to determine how it would be used for medicinal treatments. The report indicated that it contained sulfates, chlorides, iron, aluminum, and compounds of calcium and magnesium. As the Stella Niagara Campus developed, the need for water increased and the spring was examined; however, it was determined to contain too many minerals, including a high level of iron, for the facilities use. Instead, Stella Niagara installed a pump house near the river and used river water. The old pump house is still on the property.

The spring is found along Lower River Road across from the Stella Niagara campus on the newly formed twenty-nine-acre Stella Niagara Preserve on the Niagara River, protected by the Western New York Land Conservancy. There are signs indicating the preserved property. A recent discussion with the organization's conservation project manager, Dave Spiering, indicated that they are aware of the spring and are incorporating it into their restoration plans. The conservancy, which is still working on the property, welcomes visitors. As you face west, toward the river, the spring is on the right near the large stone grotto titled "Bernadette of Lourdes." The spring marsh area is thick with brush and is best viewed when the vegetation is low, although you can see the runoff in a ditch as it makes its way to the bank and flows into the Niagara. The whole area is interesting and worth exploring due to its history, walking trails, fishing, and access to the water for kayaking. Visitors are directed to the Lewiston Senior Center, with parking in the lot near the baseball fields.

J. Boles 2017
The Stella Niagara Grotto Mineral Spring is in the marsh in front of the grotto.

The small stream from the spring as it flows to the river.   *J. Boles 2017*

CHAPTER 10

The Joe Whalen Sulfur Spring
Lockport, New York

This long forgotten mineral spring was mentioned to me in 2015 by the late Joe Whalen, a famous Lockport artist. The spring was located on the northwest section of Niagara Street at the bottom of the hill, on the left just past the railroad tracks. The spring was somewhat developed, as Joe stated: "There was a covered springhouse and the mineral water was available to all." He continued, "There was a strong sulfur smell and a rotten egg taste from the spring." Although Joe did not like the water, his father was fond of it and believed it was healthy.

J. Boles 2015

Joe Whalen Sulfur Spring – northwest Niagara Street on the left side of the road.

walk over the hill from their Lock Street home in the north end and continue down Glenwood Avenue past the clear Glenwood Spring, which was water Joe liked. Glenwood had two springs: one just past the Glenwood cemetery and one where Glenwood Avenue became a dirt road, near the Michigan Street hill, which at that time continued west to Niagara Street. This was the road Joe and his father walked to the sulphur spring.

J. Boles 2015

Glenwood Spring — one of the springs Joe Whalen liked. This old, well known spring is flowing nicely.

I have searched the Niagara Street location as Joe described it—"below the hill, just past the railroad tracks"—but have not found the remains of a spring house. The area is overgrown and wet, making the discovery of the spring difficult, but I haven't given up. Also, the road, railroad crossing and the bridge over Indian Creek have been altered several times.

This spring is only a short distance upstream from the Lockport Mineral Spring, which commercially sold bottled sulfur water. Sulfur and mineral spring water, it was believed, would help the digestive process, benefit overall health, and contribute to a healthy complexion. Recent research claims that residents of countries that have a high overall sulfur intake are healthier.

I need some assistance from the readers with stories about this spring and its location. Thank you to Joe Whalen, Lockport resident Helen McGreevy, and homeowners Wally Edmister and Waylon Edmister, who both live in the Niagara Street area.

CHAPTER 11

Springs and Artesian Wells
Royalton, New York

It was May 5, 1944, and ten-year-old Ken Frey was standing in the front of Frey's Garage, his father's repair shop, in Wolcottsville, New York, when a military plane flew over low, smoking, and on fire. The plane exploded west beyond the Frey family's twenty-acre property.

Ken and his father, Roy, rushed over to the site on Route 93 and saw the remains of the Bell Cobra, which was on a test flight from Bell Aircraft. The pilot, Army Air Force Caption Lunquist, had safely parachuted. The plane crashed just behind a house, which is now 8420 Akron Road; the heavy metal landing gear and engine were buried deep in the soil.

In November 2016, Ken Frey and I went to the site of his fathers' garage and then visited the property where most of the plane finally landed. Ed and Beverly Earle, who had lived in the house for many years, knew about the crash but did not know the history. We walked the site with Ken Frey showing us what he had witnessed.

There are local stories about the site. First it is thought that Bell and military personnel were quickly working to clean up a crash site that might contain military secrets, as a war was going on. Second, the metal was buried deep, and a large hole was left, which quickly

J. Boles 2016
The site of Frey's Garage in 1944. Ken Frey demonstrates where he was when the WWII Cobra flew directly over his father's garage. It is now Frank's Garage, 6374 Wolcottsville Road, Royalton, New York.

filled up with water and reportedly was then used as a pond. The spot is now a covered mound. Locals believe that the engine is still in the ground. After a visit to the Niagara Aerospace Museum in Niagara Falls, and a discussion with the knowledgeable guides there, I'm inclined to think that rather than protecting military secrets, the officials were likely trying to determine the cause of the crash so that all the Cobras could be readied for service. Many of the Bell Cobra aircraft manufactured were sent to Russia to help their effort with the war.

The one distinctive memory that Ken Frey, now in his eighties, had about that time is not the crash itself or the excitement of the police and military personnel protecting the site; it's the artesian well that was on the property. "It flowed out of the ground making a big stream in the yard—a lot of water," he said.

Frey's story about the plane crash led me to investigate this area of Niagara County. From talking with local homeowners and remembering a previous discussion with Bill Frey from Frey Well Drilling in Alden, New York, I gathered that this section of Royalton, New York, is well known for its vigorous free-flowing artesian wells.

I do get questions about the various springs, and many are about artesian wells. The science of hydrogeology is complicated, and experts with multiple degrees devote their entire careers to understanding water. I try to keep it simple by just looking at our local conditions. This area of Niagara County has an original source of water that is found at a higher level than the top of the drilled well and sits on an aquifer that contains water under pressure. When the area is drilled for a well, the pressured water flows freely, usually from a pipe, and a pump is not needed. An area such as this one can also have seeps or lower flowing springs pushing up to the surface, which when drilled can result in a healthy artesian well.

According to Walt Van Buren, who has lived and farmed on Akron Road all his life, the land along Route 93 has many springs and artesian wells. Van Buren notes that "As you head south up 93 and onto Block Church Road, the wells are often sulfur; the water is not as good." His farmland has "good, clear water," he said.

On Grove Road, around the corner from the Van Buren farmhouse, there is a healthy spring that floods a small marsh. Nearby on Block Church Road, where it intersects with Simms Road, there is an old basin that is always gushing clear, cold sulfur water. Residents say it has always been there. This is a very active spring that fills the long drainage ditches.

Once thought of as a source of mineral water, the sulfur spring was visited by those seeking good health, according to long-time residents Donald and Shirley Walters, who live across the street. It was also a favorite of the local men who worked at Simonds Saw and Steel in Lockport, a place where they would cool off after working a long shift at the hot mill.

The water has a good taste but a heavy sulfur smell, and the basin and path of the water are painted with a white sulfur coating. It's a great example of flowing sulfur water.

J. Boles 2017

Just a short distance away, on Route 93, is an artesian well that has flowed for many years. Clear, cold water supplied a house and a business.

J. Boles 2017

Block Church Road – Sulfur Spring. Note the white sulfur coating in the basin and in the overflow pipe.

In the nineteenth and early twentieth centuries, mineral water with some sulfur content was sought in the Niagara County area for its health benefits. It was bottled and sold by the Lockport Mineral Water Company, with its spring in the Gulf, and the G.W. Merchant Company, Lockport, New York, with spring water from Oak Orchard Sour Springs in Alabama, New York. Later the Spalding Spring north of Main Street in Lockport, New York, was declared a sulfur spring and marketed by Lockport businessman J. B. Storms as Crystal Radio-Active Water.

For their help with this article, my thanks to Ken Frey, Royalton town historian Jesse Beiber, Walt Van Buren, Frank Pfalzer from Frank's Garage, Ed and Beverly Earle, Donald and Shirley Walters, the Niagara AeroSpace Museum, Wally Edmister, Vince's Auto, and Frey's Well Drilling. I am getting a number of emails and calls from local residents that are very helpful in uncovering history in Niagara County—and I welcome more!

CHAPTER 12

Springs You Can Visit in Niagara County

I have had several responses to the "Springs You Can Visit" article previously published in the *Lockport Union-Sun & Journal*. One was from Fred Lee, a former Lockport-area resident who called from Northville, a small town in the Adirondack Mountains, after a relative sent him a copy of the column. He was visiting Lockport and wanted to tell me the story of the Transit Road Spring.

I met Lee at the site on South Transit Road in front of North Buffalo Suburban Airport. As a child, Lee lived with his family on the farm that was located to the north of the spring. His father built and ran the airport. As a youngster, Lee was present when the artesian well was drilled, and he recalled that when the driller hit water, the rig blew up and flew twenty feet into the air; everyone ran for cover. They were unable to recover the drill bit—it is still in the ground. The water flowed up to ten feet for weeks and eventually settled into a healthy artesian well that was used by his family and thirsty travelers. It was mentioned that people are still drinking the water. Lee pointed out another spring that was on his parents' farm, just forty feet north of this location, and yet another that is now under the parking lot of the airport office on the corner. The house and barns from the farm are gone, but the two springs remain.

Jim Sobczyk, a Pendleton resident, directed me to this vigorous spring, which fills a deep ditch in Pendleton. The spring is about fifteen feet from South Transit Road on the west side; the nearest cross street is Dunnigan Road (and the Transit Drive-In Theatre is across the road, on the east side). Parking on Dunnigan or the nearby commercial parking lot is advised, as traffic is heavy on Transit.

Transit is one of the older roads in the area and has been widened many times. Long ago, this spring was much farther away from the road, and there was a house and a farm on the property.

Transit Road Spring. *J. Boles 2020*

The Spring on Goat Island

This is the spring after improvements; the water now ran out of an enclosed basin into a pipe. The Goat Island Spring was popular with visitors to the falls and also used by Niagara Falls Hotels when they were looking for clean water. Files of J. Boles.

J. Boles 2017

The Goat Island Spring still runs. It is located between the two bridges to the island. There is a stair to the spring on the east side of the island.

Lockport Mineral Spring

This well-documented spring is in Gulf Wilderness Park on West Jackson Street. After a short walk on the marked upper (yellow) trail, which goes to the west, you will find the remains of a commercialized mineral spring that had activity starting in the 1860s. Mineral water, which was claimed to cure many ills, was bottled and sold, and the spring was also used by Lockport residents who visited the peaceful natural valley, then named "Wood Glen." There was a proposal, just before the Civil War, to build a sanitarium in Wood Glen.

Highlighting its importance, this spring was listed in the 1886 United States Geological Survey of the Mineral Springs of the United States.

Over the years, I have interviewed older Lockport residents who remember this spring and the foundation of the spring house, and I have created a chronological history of the remains. I have not found anyone who remembers the spring house intact, but I do have a report of the remains of the wooden structure on top of the cement foundation being painted green. The foundation of the spring

Lockport Mineral Spring – Spring House Foundation.   J. Boles 2017

house now has large holes in the side that allow the water to drain into Indian Creek. Lockport resident John Coleman remembers roaming the Gulf as a youngster with his friends Ray DeNeau and Jim Johnston. The boys brought their BB guns and threw coins into the basin full of "the rotten egg water," which Coleman would not drink. At that time, there were no holes in the foundation, and the basin would fill up. South of the spring house is the carved stone bottling basin.

J. Boles 2015

Lockport Mineral Spring cut stone bottling basin, which is found on the banks of Indian Creek.

All of this is important to know as the Lockport Mineral Spring is researched. Period reports list "Wood Glen" as having two active springs. Where is the other one?

Hawley Street Spring, Lockport, New York

The Hawley Street Spring is found in the rock walls that were cut out of the escarpment to level out the hillside for the road. Now closed for many years, the north end of Hawley Street used to go down a steep hill to Glenwood Avenue. The asphalt is turning into a field, with small trees and plants growing up through the crumbling surfaces. It no longer looks like a paved street.

About halfway down the hill, to the left or west, is a rock face with a clear spring coursing through a rock channel that eventually runs down the hill. This spring has always been there, according to John Coleman, eighty-nine at the time of our talk, a longtime Hawley Street resident.

"The water was clear and good tasting … it was used for drinking, for those on a hike," Mr. Coleman told me. He also mentioned that as visitors traveled to nearby St. Patrick's Cemetery, they would stop

J. Boles 2017
Hawley Street Spring with a pile of road scrapings blocking the spring and small stream.

on Hawley to collect water for plants and flowers on the graves. Men working "over the Hill" at the factories in Lowertown would stop for a drink.

I stopped at the spring in May of 2017, but I had difficulty finding it. A large load of road scrapings now covers the spring and the rivulet that runs down the hill. Although it still flows under the pile, somewhat, it would be great to see this pile moved.

Glenwood Avenue Spring

J. Boles August 2016
This spring on Glenwood Avenue in Lockport can be seen from the road, but the last time I was there, the land was posted.

Oak Hill Spring

This spring was once on the property of Seymour Scovell. It was found below his large house, known as Oak Hill, built in 1834. Locally it is known as the Scovell/Starkweather Manson, and it is historically reported that the residents and house are the basis of the play and movie by Joseph O. Kesserling titled *Arsenic and Old Lace*. The home burned down in 1964, but the spring remains.

The spring was made into an environmental artwork by artist Peter Richards in 1989. It is easy to visit because it is in Art Park, Lewiston, New York. As you drive west into Lewiston down Main Street, turn left onto Fourth Street, park in lot D—the first lot to the right—and follow the signs that are east of the parking lot. You are looking for Oak Hill Project and Richards' Marsh. This area of Lewiston had many springs that poured into the Niagara River Gorge. At one time, there were several bottling companies along nearby Guard Street that drilled into the springs from the top of the gorge banks, bottled the mineral water, and sold it. The land was altered when the Niagara Power Project and Art Park were constructed.

I talked to artist Peter Richards in 2014, and he said the project began when the Art Park staff talked to him about developing a creation

Oak Hill Spring, Lewiston, New York.   J. Boles 2017

around the spring, which at that time was "just a drainage ditch." As we talked, Richards said he was concerned about the reports that the project had been neglected but was pleased to see a cleanup had been completed.

Other springs that can be visited are the Stella Niagara Grotto Spring (chapter nine), the Block Church Road Sulphur Spring (chapter eleven) and Wheeler Road Spring, one mile east of Transit Road (Route 78) Newfane, New York, right side of the road.

Wheeler Road Spring, Newfane, NY.   J. Boles 2020

CHAPTER 13

Are the Springs Dry?

As reported in the *Lockport Union Sun & Journal* on July 16 and August 5—and in a thorough article by Rachel Fuerschbach on August 29, 2016—there have been multiple warnings about the impact of the drought in the Western New York area. Because of this, I have received several questions from readers about our local springs. Having researched dozens of springs in Niagara County, I recently checked in on a few of them to see their condition during this very dry summer of 2016.

A healthy spring on the Niagara Escarpment before the drought – south of Route 104. Photo courtesy Falzguy 2015.

J. Boles August 2016

Vita Water Spring Bottling House, Lockport, New York, with just a trickle of water down from its reported peak of 7,200 gallons a day.

J. Boles 2016

Gulf Mineral Spring – Spring House. The Lockport Gulf Mineral Spring, which usually has a large rivulet flowing into Indian Creek, is now dry.

All the springs just below or on the escarpment receive water from the recharge area above the escarpment that flows down ground faults and fissures to discharge with some pressure at the spring. Based on past years, these springs will return to their previous output. If we have a fall with rainfall and a winter with a healthy snowfall, they will be back to normal in the spring of 2017.

CHAPTER 14

Chief Joseph Brant's Spring
"A European Military Associated Mohawk Habitation Site"
Lewiston, New York

This is a spring of mystery and legal uncertainty. Once an operational spring in the middle of a large historic Native American settlement on both sides of Ridge Road (Route 104) going west into Lewiston, New York, in the 1770s, which has been called the "Loyal Confederate Valley," it is now a loose pile of rocks buried in the brush and leaves. Joseph Brant was an officer and loyal supporter of the British in the Revolutionary War (the American War of Independence), 1775–1783, fighting for the British. The land along Ridge Road was his base for raids on areas needed for British control.

The spring is all that is left of Chief Brant's farm and the encampment area of his mostly Mohawk followers who fled from the Mohawk Valley in Central New York. The land is now a housing development—with one exception. It is reported that circa 1805, the Holland Land Company designated the land around the spring as a "park or reservation" with a right of way for public access.

Perhaps one of the smallest reservations in existence, it is roughly in feet, 295 x 193 x 173. It is a triangle on a shelf of the escarpment

Chief Brant's Farm and Settlement

The Brant farm has been described as about fifty acres and operated roughly from 1779-1785. It was six miles from Fort Niagara on Ridge Road, now route 104. The settlement included a vigorous spring, an Anglican log church, Brant's "block" house and smaller dwellings for his followers. Ownership of the property in the 1770s, during this time of war with the British before the Holland Land Company secured it is undetermined. This also a time of fluidity in claimed land ownership with Native Americans pushed off their land treaties violated, control of the land could change quickly. Although it is confusing, consulted historians believe the land rights are thought to have been included in a treaty with the Senecas, but in those unsettled times this is not clear, and the area was controlled by the British. It is thought Brant obtained the right to use the settlement land through his many British connections. As the Holland Land Company later gained control and surveyed the land a small section was set aside as a "reservation" and designated as "Brant's Spring." In the early 1800s Lemuel Cooke bought some of the land, which included the farmland and the spring. It is interesting that the spring, which at that time was vigorous and supplied the area with water, is listed in later property records as a "reservation" and as part of nearby property deeds with a right of way, which included access for a pipe that ran north down to Ridge Road.

with the housing subdivision carved around it. Maps clearly show the spring area and a right of way through the subdivision housing; however, it is not now defined in current land records as a special piece of property deserving of historical status. The definition of "reservation" from the early information is not clear. Did the Holland Land Company's designation of the spring as a "reservation" have any historical or legal significance? Does the special status still exist?

The spring area is very clearly defined in the "Report to the Town of Lewiston Planning Board," dated 1997 by McIntyre Surveying and Engineering Co., Niagara Falls, New York, in a section titled "Four Seasons Subdivision Phase 1 Approval." This report is in preparation for the development of the subdivision that bordered Brant's Spring. In summary, the report states that in a land transition in the early part of the nineteenth century the Holland Land Company preserved a permanent public right of way to the spring site.

J. Boles 2019
The path to Brant's Spring. A ray of sun finds its way through the thick trees, marking the way.

J. Boles 2019
Brant Spring — The top cap remains; there is a flowing spring beneath the rocks.

I am not comfortable disclosing the location of the spring for several reasons. Until all the concerned parties decide what the status of the spring is and find a way to protect it from harm—but still preserve it and allow appropriate visitors—the location should remain unknown. There is no protection of the site now except that it is difficult to get to and somewhat hard to find. Brant's Spring could use a rational review of its status as a historical site.

Some Native Americans consider the area sacred, and when they can, they clean up around the spring. There are accounts of Native Americans trying to visit the spring; however, this is difficult because of the uncertainty over the ownership and access. The spring is the only remainder of this Native settlement that existed during a troubling and brutal time in American History.

The other concern is the legal status of the "reservation." It is on early maps with a narrow right of way through the housing development to the spring. A 1993 letter from John W. Kohl, Chairman of the Board of R.O.L.E (Residents Organized for Lewiston-Porter's Environment, Inc.) to the Town of Lewiston Board mentions that the R.O.L.E has been able to "place" Brant's Spring as an official historical site. The letter continued with: "The information and photographs of this site given to the Department of Anthropology (University of Buffalo) ... will be forwarded to The New York State Department of Historical Sites to include "Brant's Spring" in their Register of Historical Sites. There are also records in the Lewiston Historical Society that indicate that the site was reviewed by the University of Buffalo and classified as a "Late 18th Century European Military Associated Mohawk Site."

A check with The New York State Bureau of Historical Sites indicates that Brant's Spring does not have an "official designation" with the state, although they do have it listed as a site of "archeological significance" and have a file on the site. The exact status has not been determined because the property has not gone through the official process, and no application has been submitted. The historical site office mentioned that the file is thin. They have several maps and a *Buffalo Evening News* article dated April 13, 1963, with a picture of the spring. I sent them a current picture of the spring.

I followed up with the University of Buffalo Department of Anthropology to find UB Site 2707. The University of Buffalo uses a numbered form, a checklist for collecting information about archaeological sites. Brant's Spring was number 2707. The information was brought to the university by John Kohl of Lewiston, New York. Handwritten is a note that "He is trying to save the site from destruction." Doug Perrelli, director of the Archaeological Survey and Professor of Anthropology at the University of Buffalo, was very helpful and forwarded the UB 2707 report. The UB 2707 report provided additional historical information about the spring and described a larger section of the Brant occupied land, with details and photos of Native and British artifacts found on the site.

It was mentioned that there was believed to be foundations from the log cabins and a church that were now buried.

> Information about the site brought to the attention of the Survey by a John Kohl on 5/3/93.
> 953 Ridge Road
> Lewiston, NY 14092
> # 754-2629
> He is trying to save the site from destruction

CHECKLIST FOR COMPILING INFORMATION
FOR
ARCHAEOLOGICAL SITE FILES

SITE NAME Brant Spring   UB# 2707
USGS QUAD Lewiston

Cover sheet for the University of Buffalo New York checklist #2707, presented to the Department of Anthropology, May 3, 1993.

In 1997, the Brantford Heritage Committee of Brantford, Ontario, submitted to Town of Lewiston Supervisor Thomas E. Sharp a letter expressing their concerns that the Brant's Spring would be protected from the proposed further development of the property. The letter goes on to say: "The movement of Joseph Brant and the Six Nations people, from upper New York State, through the Lewiston area to the Grand River Valley is the central story behind the formation of our community in Brantford, Ontario. The Brant's Spring represents a key surviving element of the former Six Nations settlement in the Lewiston area following the Revolutionary War." Recent email and a phone conversation with an official at the Brant Museum in Ontario indicated they were aware of the site and were interested in the ongoing history.

A review of the Town of Lewiston, New York, current property records in 2019 at the Clerk's Office does not show the site as a "reservation," and on the map it seems to be now attached to the adjacent property. However, the Brant's Spring property is still marked off with a dotted line, which could not be explained.

The right of way may not presently exist and does not seem to be in use. I have permission from a nearby landowner to enter the property, apparently the only legal way to view the spring.

Earnest Jens, 816 Hillside Drive, Lewiston, New York, whose property adjoined the "Brant Reservation," and Niagara County historian Clarence Lewis examine Brant's Spring. Archie Lowery, Buffalo Evening News, *April 13, 1963.*

Through it All the Water Flows

This faded picture from the 1960s shows the spring with cut stone walls and a large cap stone about four feet high to protect the water from leaves and other contaminants. All the stones are there that are now scattered on the ground, and the cut stone basin remains. What happened with the designation, the history?

During one of Western New York's recent dry summers, I visited Brant's Spring, and the clear water was bubbling down the hillside. Brant's Spring is considered a sacred site by some; the area is peaceful and is deserving of reverence and respect.

The above-mentioned groups and the Niagara County Historian's Office; the Town of Lewiston Clerk's Office; The Niagara County History Center; curator Terry Abrams from the Niagara County History Center; Niagara County Clerk's Office; Niagara County historian Catherine Emerson; the Town of Lewiston's Historian's Office and curator Tom Collister; Historical Association of Lewiston, New York; The Brant Museum; Doug Perrelli, University of Buffalo, New York all contributed to this research, and I thank them.

Authors Notes

This book is one in a series to be published by Vanishing Past Press. The focus is on early local history, care and healing, and residents' response to history. A book titled *No Harm Was Done: Alternative Medicine in Lockport New York* was published in October 2019 and is available at the Niagara County New York History Center and online at Amazon.com. Future books are under research, loosely titled, *The Poor Houses of Niagara County; Early Hospitals and Clinics,* and *Schools and Orphanages. The Keeley Gold Cures of New York State* is also in the works, and it takes a broader look at these 1890s addiction cures that I first wrote about in *The Gold Cure Institutes of Niagara Falls, New York* in 2013.

Readers are encouraged to contact me with further information or questions at jamesboles47@gmail.com, blog Vanishingpast.com.

Titles by Jim Boles

The books can be found at the Museum of disABILITY History, Buffalo, New York, your local bookstore and Amazon.com

No Harm was Done: Alternative Medicine in Lockport New York

Dr Skinners Remarkable School for "Colored Deaf and Dumb, and Blind Children, James M. Boles and Michael Boston

When There Were Poorhouses

The Gold Cure Institutes of Niagara Falls, NY

They Did No Harm-Alternative Medicine in Niagara Falls, NY

Abandoned History, Lockport New York 2017

Ivan the Invacar Series: children's books; superhero, disability related

Contributed

On The Edge of Town: Almshouses of Western New York -Publisher

No Offense Intended: A Directory of Historical Disability Terms -Editor

Abandoned Asylums of New England: A Photographic Journey by John Gray -Publisher, contributor

Buffalo State Hospital: A History of the Institution in Light and Shadow, published by the Museum of disABILITY History, Buffalo New York -Contributor

J.N Adams Memorial Hospital-Her Inside Voice by Char Szabo-Perricelli, published by the Museum of disABILITY History, Buffalo New York -Publisher, editor

Buffalo State Psychiatric Hospital: An Inside Report from the 1950s, by Patricia Kautz, published by the Museum of disABILITY History -Contributor

Path to the Institution: The New York State Asylum for Idiots by Thomas E. Stearns -Executive Editor

Beautiful Children: The Story of the Elm Hill School and Home for Feebleminded Children and Youth by Diana M. Katovitch -Editor

Of Grave Importance: The Restoration of Institutional Cemeteries by David Mack-Hardiman -Contributor

www.ingramcontent.com/pod-product-compliance
Lightning Source LLC
Chambersburg PA
CBHW041325110526
44592CB00021B/2831